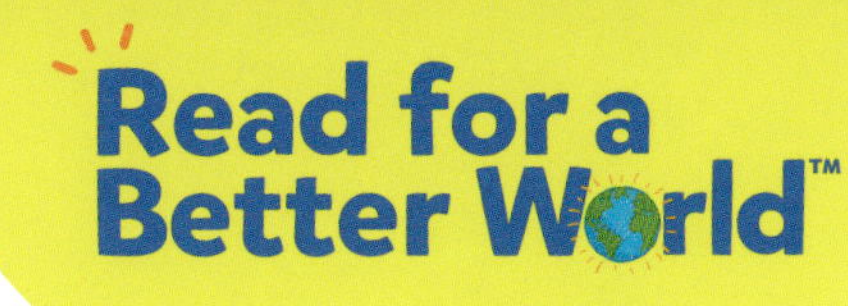

DUCKLINGS

A First Look

ANNA ANDERHAGEN

GRL Consultant, Diane Craig, Certified Literacy Specialist

Lerner Publications ◆ Minneapolis

Educator Toolbox

Reading books is a great way for kids to express what they're interested in. Before reading this title, ask the reader these questions:

What do you think this book is about? Look at the cover for clues.

What do you already know about ducklings?

What do you want to learn about ducklings?

Let's Read Together

Encourage the reader to use the pictures to understand the text.

Point out when the reader successfully sounds out a word.

Praise the reader for recognizing sight words such as *to* and *the*.

TABLE OF CONTENTS

Ducklings

Baby ducks are called ducklings. Ducklings hatch from eggs.

Ducklings stay in their nest after they are born.

They learn to walk.

Soon, they walk
to the water.
Their mom shows
them the way.

Ducklings love water.

10

They drink and swim.

Moms teach their ducklings what to eat.

Ducklings eat plants,
worms, and bugs.

Ducklings stay with their mom for two months.

Then they learn to fly!

Ducklings have
webbed feet.
They help them swim.

17

Ducklings bob their heads up and down when they are happy.

Ducks can live for ten years or more.

Ducklings love to play!

You Connect!

Have you ever seen a duckling?

What is something you like about ducklings?

What do you wear to help you swim?

STEM Snapshot

Encourage students to think and ask questions like scientists. Ask the reader:

What is something you learned about ducklings?

What is something you noticed about ducklings in the pictures in this book?

What is something you still don't know about ducklings?

Photo Glossary

Learn More

Gaertner, Meg. *Ducklings*. Lake Elmo, MN: Focus Readers, 2020.

Jaske, Julia. *Ducklings*. Ann Arbor, MI: Cherry Lake Publishing, 2022.

Rathburn, Betsy. *Baby Ducks*. Minneapolis: Bellwether Media, 2022.

Index

Photo Acknowledgments

The images in this book are used with the permission of: © Anneka/Shutterstock Images, pp. 4–5, 23 (top left); © mykhailo pavlenko/Shutterstock Images, pp. 6, 23 (top right); © Nathanial O'Connell/Shutterstock Images, p. 7; © Sheila Fitzgerald/Shutterstock Images, pp. 8–9; © JOKE_PHATRAPONG/Shutterstock Images, p. 10; © Stas Moroz/Shutterstock Images, p. 11; © K.Kargona/Shutterstock Images, pp. 12, 23 (bottom left); © Amy Lutz/Shutterstock Images, p. 13; © fotata/Shutterstock Images, p. 14; © MMCez/Shutterstock Images, p. 15; © Jaren Jai Wicklund/Shutterstock Images, pp. 16, 23 (bottom right); © Stephaniellen/Shutterstock Images, pp. 16–17; © Tomsickova Tatyana/Shutterstock Images, p. 18; © Pixel-Shot/Shutterstock Images, p. 19; © InFocus.ee/Shutterstock Images, p. 20.

Cover Photograph: © Africa Studio/Shutterstock Images

Design Elements: © Mighty Media, Inc.

Lerner Publications Company
An imprint of Lerner Publishing Group, Inc.
241 First Avenue North
Minneapolis, MN 55401 USA

For reading levels and more information, look up this title at www.lernerbooks.com.

Main body text set in Mikado a Medium.
Typeface provided by Hannes von Doehren.

Library of Congress Cataloging-in-Publication Data

Names: Anderhagen, Anna, author.
Title: Ducklings : a first look / Anna Anderhagen.
Description: Minneapolis : Lerner Publications, [2025] | Series: Read about baby animals (read for a better world) | Includes bibliographical references and index. | Audience: Ages 5-8 | Audience: Grades K-1 | Summary: "Ducklings have special feet that help them swim, which is great because they love the water. Full-color photographs and engaging text help young readers learn more about adorable baby ducks"—Provided by publisher.
Identifiers: LCCN 2023034371 (print) | LCCN 2023034372 (ebook) | ISBN 9798765626368 (library binding) | ISBN 9798765629482 (paperback) | ISBN 9798765636602 (epub)
Subjects: LCSH: Ducklings—Juvenile literature.
Classification: LCC QL696.A52 A53 2025 (print) | LCC QL696.A52 (ebook) | DDC 598.4/11392—dc23/eng/20231108

LC record available at https://lccn.loc.gov/2023034371
LC ebook record available at https://lccn.loc.gov/2023034372

Manufactured in the United States of America
1 – CG – 7/15/24